WOLFGANG AMADEUS MOZART

SYMPHONY

C major/C-Dur/Ut majeur
K 551
"Jupiter"

Edited by/Herausgegeben von
Stefan de Haan

Ernst Eulenburg Ltd
London · Mainz · Madrid · New York · Paris · Prague · Tokyo · Toronto · Zürich

CONTENTS/INHALT

Ernst Eulenburg Ltd
48 Great Marlborough Street
London W1V 2BN

PREFACE/VORWORT

The Symphony in C, K551 ('Jupiter'), was completed on 10 August 1788. Its entry in the chronological list *Verzeichnüß aller meiner Werke* that Mozart kept from February 1784 until November 1791 immediately follows that for the Symphony in G minor, K550, on 25 July. Only a few weeks earlier on 26 June the Symphony in E flat, K543, appears. In the course of little more than six weeks Mozart had written three symphonies which together with the 'Prague' Symphony of December 1786 represent his outstanding contributions to this form.

Of Mozart's sixty or so symphonies most were composed before he left the service of the Archbishop of Salzburg in May 1781. As a free-lance composer in his early Vienna years, Mozart was more interested in producing piano concertos, of which he wrote no less than fifteen between 1782 and the end of 1786, for public performance by himself or his pupil Babette Ployer. During the same period he wrote only three symphonies. The first of these in D, K385, was composed at the urgent request of his father at the end of July 1782 for the celebrations in Salzburg on the occasion of the ennoblement of Sigmund Haffner, Mozart's friend and contemporary; the second in C, K425, was written in Linz in 1783 in the space of five days for a concert on 4 November; the third in D, K504, was completed on 6 December 1786 for performance in Prague in the following January.

Am 16. August 1788 hatte Mozart die Sinfonie in C-Dur, KV 551 („Jupiter-Sinfonie") beendet. Ihre Eintragung in das chronologisch angelegte „Verzeichnüß aller meiner Werke", das er von Februar 1784 bis November 1791 führte, erfolgte unmittelbar auf die der g-Moll-Sinfonie, KV 550, die am 25. Juli in das Verzeichnis aufgenommen worden war. Nur wenige Wochen zuvor, nämlich am 26. Juni, war die Sinfonie in Es-Dur, KV 543, erschienen. Innerhalb von kaum mehr als 6 Wochen hatte Mozart somit drei Sinfonien komponiert, die zusammen mit der „Prager" Sinfonie vom Dezember 1786 beweisen, welch großartigen Beitrag Mozart zu dieser Musikgattung geleistet hat.

Die meisten seiner etwa 60 Sinfonien hatte er komponiert, bevor er im Mai 1781 aus den Diensten des Erzbischofs von Salzburg ausschied. Mozart war am Anfang seiner Zeit der freischaffenden Tätigkeit eher auf die Komposition von Klavierkonzerten ausgerichtet, von denen er zwischen 1782 und 1786 auch nicht weniger als 15 schrieb. Diese wurden von ihm selbst oder aber von seiner Schülerin Babette Ployer öffentlich aufgeführt. In diesen Jahren komponierte Mozart nur drei Sinfonien. Die erste, die Sinfonie in D-Dur, KV 385, schrieb er auf Drängen seines Vaters Ende Juli 1782 anläßlich der Feierlichkeiten, im Rahmen derer Sigmund Haffner, Mozarts Zeitgenosse und Freund, in Salzburg in den Adelsstand erhoben wurde. Die zweite Sinfonie in C-Dur, KV 425, schuf er 1783 in Linz in nur 5 Tagen, und zwar für ein Konzert, das am 4. November selbigen Jahres stattfand. Die Arbeiten an der dritten in D-Dur, KV 504, waren

It is not known for what occasions Mozart wrote his last three symphonies: they may have been intended for performance at the series of concerts he planned to give in Vienna in the summer of 1788 but this project fell through and subsequently Mozart gave no more public concerts in Vienna. Clearly it would have been quite contrary to Mozart's normal practice to have composed three large-scale works with no prospect of their being played, and even if the immediate plans for their performance had to be abandoned, it is likely that some opportunity would have been found for them to be heard at a later date. One such opportunity may have occurred during the German tour which Mozart undertook with his friend Prince Karl Lichnowsky in April and May 1789. The concert of Mozart's music given in Leipzig on 12 May 1789 may well have included one or two of his last three symphonies or at any rate some movements from them. It is possible, too, that the 'Jupiter' Symphony was one of the two symphonies due to be performed at the concert given on 15 October 1790 when Mozart was in Frankfurt for the coronation of Leopold II: in the event the programme proved to be too long, and only one of the symphonies, and that an early one, was performed. Again, the 'Jupiter' may have been the 'Grand Symphony composed by Herr Mozart' included in the 'Grand Musical Concert' given in Vienna on 16 April 1791, in a programme repeated on the 17th by the Society of Musicians. However, as on this occasion the orchestra included Mozart's clarinettist friend Anton Stadler and his brother Johann, the symphony is more likely to have been the G minor in its clarinet version or the Symphony in E

am 6. Dezember 1786 abgeschlossen; sie war für ein Konzert im darauffolgenden Januar in Prag vorgesehen.

Wir wissen nicht, zu welchem Anlaß Mozart jeweils seine letzten drei Sinfonien komponierte. Möglicherweise waren sie für eine für den Sommer 1788 in Wien geplante Konzertreihe gedacht. Diese Pläne zerschlugen sich jedoch, und so kam es, daß Mozart von diesem Zeitpunkt an in Wien keine öffentlichen Konzerte mehr gab. Dabei entsprach es durchaus nicht seiner Art, gleich drei Werke einer solchen Dimension zu komponieren, ohne daß Aussicht auf eine Aufführung bestanden hätte. Und mußten auch die Pläne für eine sich unmittelbar anschließende Aufführung aufgegeben werden, so ist doch anzunehmen, daß es zu einem späteren Zeitpunkt noch dazu kam. Eine solche Gelegenheit bot sich vielleicht bei Mozarts Reise durch Deutschland, die er im April/Mai 1789 mit seinem Freund Karl Lichnowsky unternahm. Durchaus möglich ist auch, daß eine bzw. zwei seiner letzten drei Sinfonien – zumindest aber einige Sätze hieraus – bei einem Mozart-Konzert am 12. Mai 1789 in Leipzig gespielt wurden, oder aber daß die „Jupiter-Sinfonie" zu den zwei Sinfonien gehörte, die für ein Konzert am 15. Oktober anläßlich der Krönungsfeierlichkeiten für Leopold II., zu denen Mozart nach Frankfurt gekommen war, vorgesehen waren. Das Programm erwies sich jedoch als für diesen Anlaß zu lang, und folglich wurde lediglich eine Mozart-Sinfonie, noch dazu eine seiner frühen Kompositionen, aufgeführt. Denkbar ist auch, daß es sich bei der „Großen Sinfonie von der Erfindung des Herrn Mozart", die Teil eines Programms der „Großen Musikakademie" war, die am 16. April 1791 in Wien stattfand und einen Tag später, am 17. April, von der „Tonkünstler-Sozietät" erneut angeboten wurde, um

flat, K543, which also includes clarinets in its score.

There can be no certainty about the origin of the title 'Jupiter' by which this work is now universally known. Mozart's son, Franz Xaver, told Vincent and Mary Novello on their visit to Salzburg in 1829 that it was first used by Salomon, the violinist and orchestral leader responsible for Haydn's London visits, who died in 1815.[1] Certainly the nickname was known in London in the early years of the nineteenth century: it appears in the programme of a concert given by the Philharmonic Society in March 1821 and Clementi used it in 1822 for the publication of his arrangement of the work for 'Pianoforte with accompaniments for a Flute, Violin and Violoncello'. The engraved title-page bore a splendid picture of the god seated amid the storm-clouds.[2] Tovey considered the title 'Jupiter' along with 'Emperor' and 'Moonlight' to be 'among the silliest injuries

[1] Rosemary Hughes (Ed.), *A Mozart Pilgrimage. Being the Travel Diaries of Vincent & Mary Novello in the year 1829*, transcribed and compiled by Nerina Medici di Marignano, London 1955, p.99

[2] A. Hyatt King, *Mozart in Retrospect*, London 1955, Pl. I

die „Jupiter-Sinfonie" gehandelt hat. Bedenkt man jedoch, daß zu den damaligen Orchestermitgliedern auch Mozarts Freund, der Klarinettist Anton Stadler, sowie dessen Bruder Johann zählten, so ist wohl eher davon auszugehen, daß die „Klarinettenfassung" der Sinfonie in g-Moll oder aber die Sinfonie in Es-Dur, KV 543, die ebenfalls mit Klarinetten besetzt ist, vorgetragen wurden.

Worin der Titel „Jupiter-Sinfonie", unter dem das Werk inzwischen allgemein bekannt ist, letztendlich seinen Ursprung hat, läßt sich nicht mit Bestimmtheit sagen. Bei ihrem Besuch in Salzburg im Jahre 1829 erzählte Mozarts Sohn Franz Xaver dem Ehepaar Vincent und Mary Novello, daß der 1815 verstorbene Violinist und Konzertmeister Salomon, auf dessen Einladung auch Haydns Londoner Aufenthalte zurückzuführen sind, den Titel zuerst gebraucht habe. Ganz sicher aber war der Beiname „Jupiter" bereits in den Anfangsjahren des 19. Jahrhunderts in London bekannt, denn zum einen erscheint er auf dem Programm eines Konzertes der Philharmonic Society im März 1821, zum anderen benutzte Clementi den Titel für die Veröffentlichung seiner Bearbeitung des Werkes für „Pianoforte with accompaniments for a Flute, Violin and Violincello"[1]. Der Druck auf der Titelseite zeigte das prächtige Abbild eines inmitten von Sturmwolken thronenden Gottes[2]. Für Tovey war der Titel „Jupiter", zusammen mit der in England für das 5. Klavierkonzert von Beethoven geläufigen Bezeichnung „Emperor" und dem Titel „Mondscheinsonate", „eine

[1] Rosemary Hughes (Hg.), *A Mozart Pilgrimage. Being the Travel Diaries of Vincent & Mary Novello in the year 1829*, übertragen and zusammengestellt von Nerina Medici di Marignano, London 1955, S. 99

[2] A. Hyatt King, *Mozart in Retrospect*, London 1955, Abb. I

ever inflicted on great works of art'.[3] It is true that in so wide-ranging a work there is bound to be much to which the name 'Jupiter', with its suggestion of majesty, grandeur and triumph, is not easily applicable, yet the character of much of its material, not least in the finale, and still more the heroic way in which the work as a whole turns its back on the tragic intensity of the G-minor Symphony, written less than three weeks earlier, make its now inseparable title not wholly inappropriate.

It is in fact from the fusion of its contrasting elements into a compelling unity that one of the chief glories of this symphony derives. From the very opening bars, whose conventional *f* summons from the whole orchestra is balanced by the pleading *p* answer from the strings, this reconciliation of opposites permeates the whole work. Later in the same movement, after the warm expressiveness of the second subject, and just at the very moment when the first section of the movement might be expected to reach its close, there comes tripping in a charming dancing tune straight from the world of *opera buffa*. Indeed it is an arietta, *Un bacio di mano*, that Mozart wrote three months earlier for insertion in Anfossi's opera *Le gelosie fortunate*. Not only does its appearance at this moment seem wholly appropriate, but in a characteristically Mozartian way it turns out that it is this light-hearted idea in conjunction with the 'throw-away line' of its cadence-formula that contributes substantially to the discussion in the middle section of the movement.

[3] D. F. Tovey, *Essays in Musical Analysis*, London 1935, Vol. I, p. 195

der albernsten Beleidigungen, die ein großes Kunstwerk jemals erfahren hatte"[3]. Zugegeben, ein so umfassendes Werk enthält natürlich vieles, auf das sich der Begriff „Jupiter" – Würde, Erhabenheit und Triumph suggerierend – nicht ohne weiteres anwenden läßt; was jedoch diesen Titel nicht völlig fehl am Platz erscheinen läßt, ist der Charakter des musikalischen Materials gerade im Finale und in noch stärkerem Maße die heroische Art und Weise, auf die sich das Werk von der tragisch anmutenden Intensität der Gefühle der nur kaum 3 Wochen zuvor geschriebenen g-Moll-Sinfonie abwendet.

In der Tat liegt die fundamentale Stärke der „Jupiter-Sinfonie" in der Verschmelzung der kontrastierenden Elemente zu einer zwingenden Einheit. Als Eröffnung des Satzes der konventionelle *forte*-Auftakt des gesamten Orchesters, der durch die flehentliche Erwiderung der Streicher in *piano* begütigt wird; diese Versöhnung der Gegensätze durchdringt das gesamte Werk. An späterer Stelle im selben Satz dann – das innige, *espressivo* vorgetragene zweite Thema ist gerade verklungen – und just zu einem Zeitpunkt, da der Hörer glaubt, der erste Abschnitt dieses Satzes nähere sich seinem Ende, setzt dann plötzlich „trippelnd" eine heitere tänzerische Melodie ein, die unmittelbar der Welt der opera buffa entsprungen zu sein scheint. Mozart hatte nämlich 3 Monate zuvor für Anfossis Oper *Le gelosie fortunate* tatsächlich eine Arietta mit dem Titel *Un bacio di mano* geschrieben. Nicht nur, daß das Einsetzen einer solchen Melodie an dieser Stelle völlig angemessen erscheint; auf typisch Mozartsche Weise stellt es sich auch heraus, daß besonders dieser heitere

[3] D. F. Tovey, *Essays in Musical Analysis*, London 1935, Bd. I, S. 195

What greater contrast of mood could there be than that between the jubilant ending of the first movement and the deeply felt *Andante cantabile* which follows? The muted strings lend a subdued colour to the whole movement, whose generally calm meditative flow is from time to time disturbed by passionate episodes of syncopated uneasy rhythms, sudden *fp* thrusts and adventurous chromatic harmony: and always Mozart's readiness to reject regularity of phrase-length or rigidity of bar-structure impels the music forward in a gentle but irresistible progress to its ending in a delightful coda, apparently added as an afterthought by the composer.[4] The Minuet recaptures the mood of the first movement and its Trio hints at the opening subject of the finale. The last movement is dominated by a feeling of exhilaration springing not least from the sheer mastery of Mozart's handling of his contrapuntal resources. Among the instrumental works of his maturity only in the finale of the G major String Quartet, K387, of 1782 is there the same confident deployment of fugal elements within a sonata-form movement. Here in the 'Jupiter' the music drives forward through all its variety of instrumentation and dynamic levels with boundless energy and effortless inevitability. At the coda comes a sudden momentary break in the onward flow succeeded by a few bars of stillness and reflection. Then follows a superb *fugato* combining in a contrapuntal *tour de force* all the thematic constituents of the movement, before a triumphant fanfare concludes the work. It is hard to

[4] Hermann Abert, *W. A. Mozart*, Leipzig [7]1956, Vol. II, p. 495

Einfall und die „Beiläufigkeit" der Kadenz so wesentlich zum Zwiegespräch der Instrumente in der Mitte dieses Satzes beitragen.

Es könnte wohl kaum ein größerer Stimmungsgegensatz bestehen als der zwischen dem vor Freude sprühenden Ende des ersten Satzes und dem darauf folgenden, tief empfundenen *Andante cantabile*. Die gedämpften Streicher verleihen dem gesamten Satz, dessen im allgemeinen ruhig-meditativer Fluß gelegentlich durch leidenschaftliche episodische Abschnitte synkopierter, drängender Rhythmen, unvermittelte *fp*-Stellen und gewagte chromatische Harmonik durchbrochen wird, eine dumpfe Färbung. Dabei treibt Mozarts stets vorhandene Bereitschaft, die Regelmäßigkeit der Periodik sowie das starre Schema der Taktstruktur aufzugeben, die Musik auf sanfte, doch beharrliche Weise vorwärts, bis diese in einer bezaubernden Coda – vom Komponisten offenbar als nachträglicher Einfall hinzugefügt[4] – endet. Das Menuett greift die Stimmung des ersten Satzes wieder auf, wobei das Trio auf das Eröffnungsthema des Finales hinweist. Der letzte Satz wird beherrscht von einem Gefühl der Beschwingtheit, das nicht zuletzt durch Mozarts meisterliches Können in der kontrapunktischen Verarbeitung vermittelt wird. Von den Instrumentalwerken seiner reiferen Jahre weist nur das Finale des G-Dur-Streichquartetts, KV 387, das er 1782 geschrieben hat, einen ähnlich sicheren Griff bei der Verwendung von Fugenelementen in einem im übrigen sonatenförmigen Satz auf. Hier bei der „Jupiter-Sinfonie" drängt die Musik unter Aufbietung sämtlicher instrumentaler und dynamischer Varianten mit ungezügelter Kraft und einer spieler-

[4] Hermann Abert, *W. A. Mozart*, Leipzig [7]1956, Bd. II, S. 495

imagine a more splendid ending, not only to the 'Jupiter' itself, but to the whole series of symphonies of which this was destined to be the last.

Ronald Woodham

ischen Unweigerlichkeit nach vorn. In der Coda wird dieser unaufhaltsame Fluß dann unvermittelt für einen Augenblick unterbrochen, worauf einige Takte der Stille und Reflexion folgen. Es setzt nun ein großartiges Fugato ein, das in einer kontrapunktischen ,,Tour de force" sämtliche thematischen Elemente zu einer Einheit verbindet, bevor das Werk mit einer triumphalen Fanfare beendet wird. Ein überwältigenderer Schlußpunkt – nicht nur für die ,,Jupiter-Sinfonie", sondern auch für die ganze Sinfonien-Gruppe, deren letztes Glied sie sein sollte – laßt sich nur schwerlich denken.

Ronald Woodham
Übersetzung Gabriele Vogt

Editorial Notes

This edition of K551 is based on the text of the *Neue Mozart-Ausgabe* IV/11.9 edited by H.C. Robbins Landon, published in 1957. Sources for the *NMA* included a facsimile of the autograph score, first and early editions of the score and parts, and the former Eulenburg edition (1930) by Theodore Kroyer. For the present edition however further revisions have been made and the number of *NMA* editorial insertions reduced. For example, in certain instances where Mozart wrote staccato dots for the first appearance only of a recurring figure, editorial dots are not added in later appearances (cf. II, bars 7–10, Vl. I/II) and where Mozart indicated *f* in wind parts but did not repeat the indication after several bars rest editorial *fortes* have been considered unnecessary. On the other hand, where such indications, and also slurs, are inconsistent in parallel passages they have been left as they appear in the autograph. Doubtful *NMA* editorials have also been omitted, e.g.

Revisionsbericht

Die vorliegende Ausgabe der Sinfonie KV 551 beruht auf dem Text der 1957 erschienenen *Neuen Mozart Ausgabe* IV/ 11.9, herausgegeben von H.C. Robbins Landon. Als Quelle für die *NMA* dienten u.a. ein Faksimile der autographen Partitur, die Erstausgabe sowie weitere frühe Ausgaben von Partitur und Stimmen, und schließlich die frühere Eulenburg-Ausgabe (1930) Theodor Kroyers. Die vorliegende Ausgabe stellt jedoch eine erneute Überarbeitung dar, in der die Anmerkungen der *NMA*-Herausgeber zahlenmäßig verringert werden. Wo Mozart beispielsweise Staccato-Punkte nur beim ersten Auftreten einer wiederkehrenden Figur angab, werden diese von den Herausgebern bei späterem Wiederauftreten ebenfalls weggelassen (vgl. II. Satz, Takte 7–10, Vl. I/II). Ebenso erschien es den Herausgebern überflüssig, *forte* anzugeben, wo ein von Mozart den Bläsern vorgegebenes *f* nach einigen Takten Pause nicht erneut vorgeschrieben wurde. Dort wo diese An-

the high G trill for bassoon in I, bar 65, which Mozart may have intentionally excluded for technical reasons. The problems posed in interpreting Mozart's staccato signs is well known to editors.[5] Reliance for this edition on the *NMA*, which seeks to preserve the distinction between the stroke and dot, entails the acceptance of Robbins Landon's judgement on the text.

All editorial additions are clearly indicated within square brackets or by dotted ties and slurs.

[5] For a full discussion see Hans Albrecht (Ed.), *Die Bedeutung der Zeichen Keil, Strich und Punkt bei Mozart*, Kassel 1957

gaben, auch in bezug auf Legatobögen, in parallelen Abschnitten jedoch uneinheitlich sind, wurden sie so belassen, wie sie im Autograph erscheinen. In der *NMA* zweifelhafte editorische Anmerkungen, wie zum Beispiel im I. Satz/Takt 65 der hohe G-Triller des Fagotts, den Mozart aus technischen Gründen absichtlich nicht angegeben haben könnte, wurden ebenfalls weggelassen. Die Herausgeber sind sich der Probleme, die sich bei der Interpretation von Mozarts Staccato-Zeichen ergeben, durchaus bewußt[5]. Indem sich diese Ausgabe an die der *NMA* anlehnt, die an der Unterscheidung zwischen Strich und Punkt festzuhalten sucht, schließt sie sich den Beurteilungen Robbins Landons zum Notentext an.

Sämtliche Ergänzungen des Herausgebers sind deutlich durch eckige Klammern bzw. gestrichelte Bögen gekennzeichnet.

[5] Eine umfassende Diskussion bringt Hans Albrecht (Hg.), *Die Bedeutung der Zeichen Keil, Strich und Punkt bei Mozart*, Kassel 1957

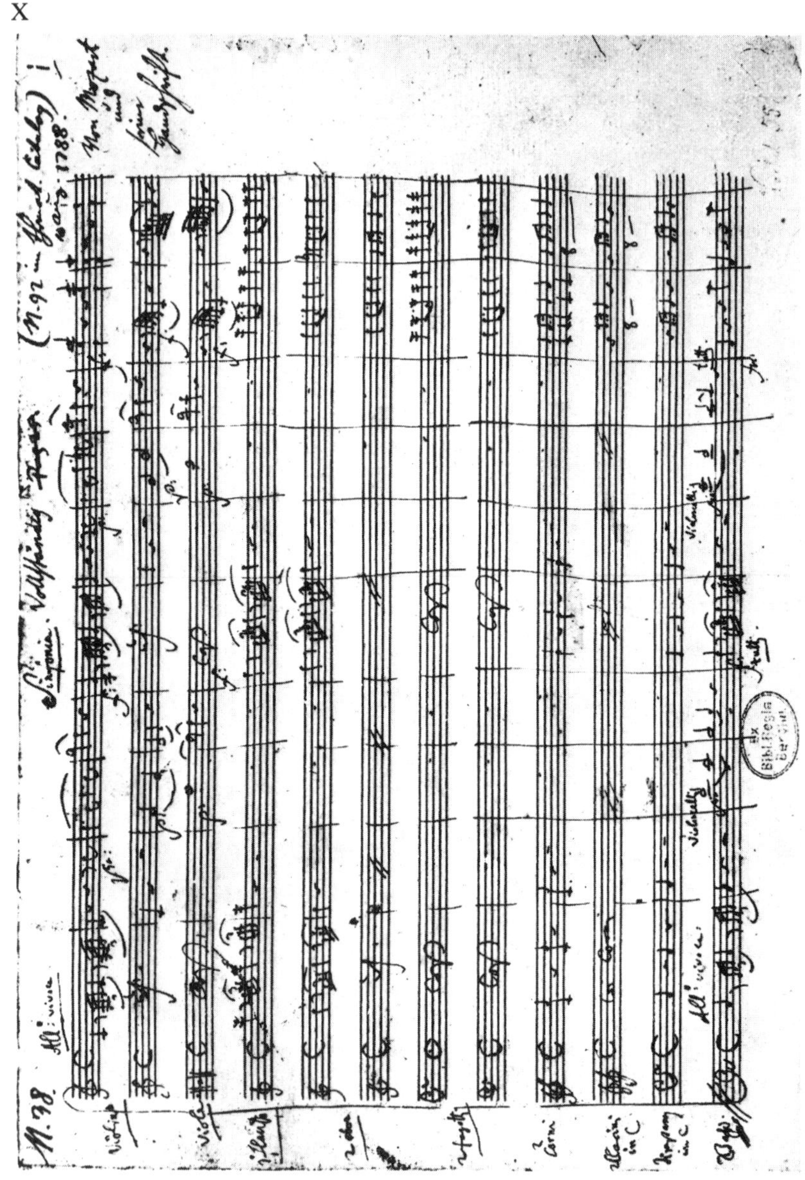

First page from the autograph score
Erste Seite aus dem Autograph der Partitur

SYMPHONY

Wolfgang Amadeus Mozart
(1756–1791)
K 551
I. Allegro vivace
Flauto
Oboe 1 2
Fagotto 1 2
Corno (C) 1 2
Tromba (C) 1 2
Timpani (C.G)
Violino I II
Viola
Violoncello e Contrabasso
a2
Vc.
tutti
Fl.
Ob.
Fg.
Cor. (C)
Tr. (C)
Timp.
Vl.
Vla.
Vc. Cb.

12
Fl.
Ob.
Fg.
Cor.(C)
Tr. (C)
Timp.
Vl.
Vla.
Vc.
Cb.
17
Fl.
Ob.
a2
Fg.
a2
Cor. (C)
a2
Tr. (C)
a2
Timp.
Vl.
Vla.
Vc.
Cb.

24
Fl.
Ob.
Fg.
or.(C)
Vl.
30
Fl.
Ob.
Fg.
Vl.
Vla.
Vc.
Cb.
Vc.

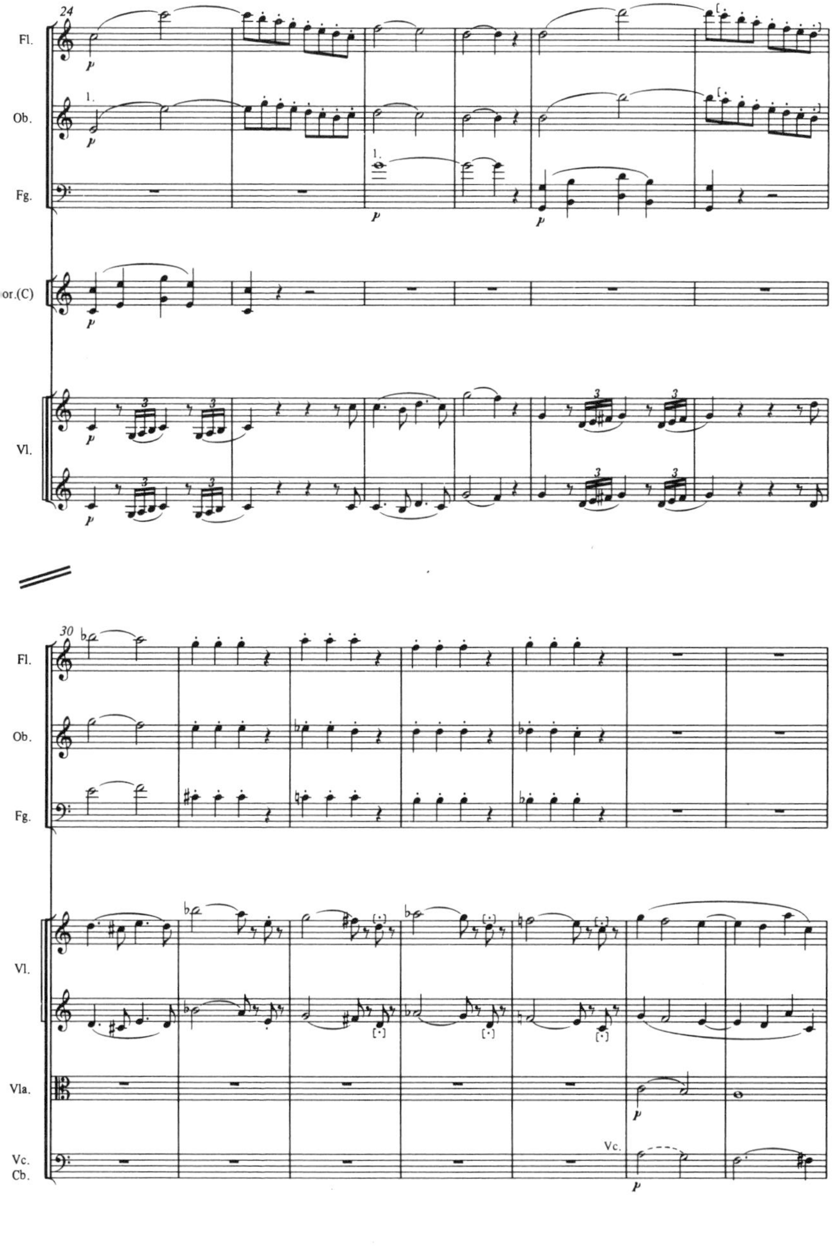

37
Fl.
Ob.
Fg.
Cor.(C)
Tr. (C)
Timp.
Vl.
Vla.
Vc.
Cb.
a2
tutti
Vc.
Cb.
43
Fl.
Ob.
Fg.
Cor. (C)
Tr. (C)
Timp.
Vl.
Vla.
Vc.
Cb.
tutti

49
Fl.
Ob.
Fg.
Vl.
Vla.
Vc.
Cb.
54
Fl.
Ob.
Fg.
(C)
(C)
Vl.
Vla.
Vc.
Cb.

59
Fg.
1.
p
Vl.
Vla.
Vc.
Cb.
64
Fl.
Fg.
p
Vl.
Vla.
Vc.
Cb.
69
Fl.
Fg.
Vl.
Vla.
Vc.
Cb.

74
Vl.
Vla.
Vc.
Cb.
81
Fl.
Ob.
Fg.
Cor. (C)
Tr. (C)
Timp.
Vl.
Vla.
Vc.
Cb.

88

Fl.

Ob.

Fg.

Cor. (C)

Tr. (C)

Timp.

Vl.

Vla.

Vc.
Cb.

a2 a2 a2 a2

Vc. Cb.

sf sf

93

Fl.

Ob.

Fg.

Cor.(C)

Tr. (C)

Timp.

Vl.

Vla.

Vc.
Cb.

a2 a2

tutti

98
Fl.
Ob.
Fg.
Cor. (C)
Tr. (C)
Vl.
Vla.
Vc.
Cb.
a2
pizz.
arco
104
1.
tutti
pizz.

109
Fl.
Ob.
Fg.
Cor. (C)
Tr. (C)
Vl.
Vla.
Vc.
Cb.
113
Fl.
Ob.
Fg.
Cor.(C)
Tr. (C)
Vl.
Vla.
Vc.
Cb.

117
Fl.
Ob.
Fg.
Cor.(C)
Tr. (C)
Timp.
[f]
Vl.
Vla.
Vc.
Cb.
121
p
1.
pizz.
arco
Vc.
Cb.
pizz.
[sim.]

127
Fl.
Ob.
1.
Fg.
1.
Vl.
Vla.
Vc.
Cb.
tutti
pizz.
132
Fl.
f
Ob.
1.
f
Fg.
1.
f
Vl.
f
f
Vla.
arco
f
Vc.
Cb.
arco
f

137
Fl.
Ob.
Fg.
Vl.
Vla.
Vc.
Cb.
142
Fl.
Ob.
a2
Fg.
a2
Vl.
Vla.
Vc.
Cb.

147
Fl.
Ob.
Fg.
Vl.
Vla.
Vc.
Cb.
152
p
1.

157
Fl.
Ob.
1.
Fg.
p
Vl.
Vla.
Vc.
Vc.
Cb.
p
tutti
p
162
Fl.
p
2.
Ob.
p
1.
Fg.
Cor.(C)
p
Vl.
Vla.
Vc.
Cb.

167
Fl.
Ob.
1.
Fg.
Vl.
Vla.
Vc.
Cb.
171
Fl.
Ob.
Fg.
Cor.(C)
Tr. (C)
Timp.
Vl.
Vla.
Vc.
Cb.

175
Fl.
Ob.
Fg.
Cor.(C)
Tr. (C)
Timp.
Vl.
Vla.
Vc.
Cb.
179
a 2
p
p
p

183
Fl.
Ob.
Fg.
Cor.(C)
Tr. (C)
Timp.
Vl.
Vla.
Vc.
Cb.
1.
Vc.
188
a2
tutti

194
Fl.
Ob.
Fg.
Cor. (C)
Tr. (C)
Timp.
Vl.
Vla.
Vc.
Cb.
p
Vc.
f
tutti
200

205
Fl.
Ob.
a2
Fg.
a2
Cor.(C)
a2
Tr. (C)
a2
Timp.
Vl.
Vla.
Vc.
Cb.
212
Fl.
p
Ob.
1.
p
Fg.
p
1.
Vl.
p
p
Vla.
p
Vc.
Cb.
Vc.

217
Fl.
Ob.
1.
Fg.
Cor.(C)
p
Vl.
Vla.
Vc.
Vc.
Cb.
222
Fl.
Ob.
Fg.
1.
a2
Cor.(C)
Tr. (C)
Timp.
f
Vl.
Vla.
Vc.
Cb.
tutti
3

227
Fl.
a2
Ob.
Fg.
Cor.(C)
Tr. (C)
Timp.
Vl.
Vla.
Vc.
Vc.
Cb.
Cb.
234
Fl.
Ob.
Fg.
Cor.(C)
a2
Tr. (C)
a2
Timp.
Vl.
Vla.
tutti
Vc.
Cb.

239
Fl.
Ob.
Fg.
Cor.(C)
Tr. (C)
Timp.
Vl.
Vla.
Vc.
Cb.
244
p
[tr]
248
1.

253
Fl.
Ob.
Fg.
Cor.(C)
Vl.
Vla.
Vc.
Cb.
258
Fl.
Ob.
Fg.
Cor.(C)
Vl.
Vla.
Vc.
Cb.

263
Fl.
Ob.
Fg.
Cor.(C)
Vl.
Vla.
Vc.
Cb.
269
Tr. (C)
Timp.
a2

276
Fl.
Ob.
Fg.
Cor. (C)
Tr. (C)
Timp.
Vl.
Vla.
Vc.
Cb.
sf
281
a2
a2

286
Fl.
Ob.
Fg.
Cor.(C)
Tr. (C)
Timp.
Vl.
Vla.
Vc.
Cb.
pizz.
arco
292
[sim.]
tutti

297
Fl.
Ob.
Fg.
1.
p
a2
f
Cor.(C)
Tr. (C)
Timp.
Vl.
Vla.
arco
Vc.
Cb.
301
tr

305
Fl.
Ob.
Fg.
Cor. (C)
Tr. (C)
Timp.
Vl.
Vla.
Vc.
Cb.
309
a2
a2
tr

II. Andante cantabile

10
Fl.
1.
Fg.
Cor.(F)
Vl.
Vla.
Vc.
Cb.
13
Fg.
Cor.(F)
Vl.
Vla.
Vc.
Cb.

17
Fl.
Ob.
Fg.
Cor.(F)
Vl.
Vla.
Vc.
Cb.
21
Fl.
Ob.
Fg.
Cor.(F)
Vl.
Vla.
Vc.
Cb.

24
Fl.
Ob.
Fg.
Cor.(F)
Vl.
Vla.
Vc.
Cb.
1.
28
a2

31
Fl.
Ob.
Fg.
Cor.(F)
Vl.
Vla.
Vc.
Cb.
34
Fl.
Ob.
Fg.
Vl.
Vla.
Vc.
Cb.

37
Fl.
Ob.
Fg.
Cor. (F)
Vl.
Vla.
Vc.
Cb.
cresc.
f
39
p
1.
[p]

42
Fl.
1.
Ob.
Fg.
Cor.(F)
Vl.
Vla.
Vc.
Cb.
45
Fl.
cresc.
sfp
Ob.
cresc.
sfp
Fg.
cresc.
sfp
Cor.(F)
cresc.
sfp
Vl.
cresc.
f
p
Vla.
f
p
Vc.
Cb.
f
p

57
Fl.
Ob.
1.
Fg.
Cor.(F)
Vl.
Vla.
Vc.
Cb.
60
Fl.
Ob.
Fg.
Cor.(F)
f
[p]
Vl.
Vla.
Vc.
Cb.

63
Fg.
Cor.(F)
Vl.
Vla.
Vc.
Cb.
f
66
Fl.
Ob.
Fg.
a 2
Cor.(F)
Vl.
Vla.
Vc.
Cb.
p
f

68
Fl.
Ob.
Fg.
Cor.(F)
Vl.
Vla.
Vc.
Cb.
70
Fl.
Ob.
Fg.
Cor.(F)
Vl.
Vla.
f [f]
Vc.
Cb.
ff

72
Fl.
Ob.
Fg.
Cor.(F)
Vl.
Vla.
Vc.
Cb.
75
Fl.
Ob.
Fg.
Cor.(F)
Vl.
Vla.
Vc.
Cb.

78
Fl.
Ob.
1.
Fg.
Cor.(F)
Vl.
Vla.
Vc.
Cb.
81
Fl.
Ob.
Fg.
Cor.(F)
Vl.
Vla.
Vc.
Cb.

84
Fl.
Ob.
Fg.
Cor.(F)
Vl.
Vla.
Vc.
Cb.
cresc.
f
87
p
1.
[p]

90
Fl.
Ob.
Fg.
Cor. (F)
Vl.
Vla.
Vc.
Cb.
[p]
93
p
1.
a 2
f

96
Fl.
Ob.
Fg.
Cor.(F)
Vl.
Vla.
Vc.
Cb.
p
1.
99
pp

III. Menuetto

13
Fl.
Ob.
Fg.
Cor.(C)
Tr. (C)
Timp.
Vl.
Vla.
Vc.
Cb.
tutti
21
a2

29
Fl.
Ob.
Fg.
Cor.(C)
Tr. (C)
Timp.
Vl.
Vla.
Vc.
Cb.
a2
a2
a2
a2
36
Fl.
Ob.
Fg.
Cor.(C)
Tr. (C)
Timp.
Vl.
Vla.
Vc.
Cb.

44
Fl.
Ob.
Fg.
Cor.(C)
Tr. (C)
Timp.
Vl.
Vla.
Vc.
Cb.
1.
a2
53
tutti
[Fine]

Trio
60
Fl.
Ob.
Fg.
Cor.(C)
Vl.
Vla.
Vc.
Cb.
68
Fl.
Ob.
Fg.
Cor.(C)
Tr. (C)
Vl.
Vla.
Vc.
Cb.

74
Fl.
Ob.
Fg.
Cor.(C)
Tr. (C)
Vl.
Vla.
Vc.
Cb.
81
[Menuetto D.C. al Fine]

IV. [Finale]

Molto Allegro
Flauto
Oboe 1 2
Fagotto 1 2
Corno (C) 1 2
Tromba (C) 1 2
Timpani (C.G)
Violino I
Violino II
Viola
Violoncello e Contrabasso
Fl.
Ob.
Fg.
Cor. (C)
Tr. (C)
Timp.
Vl.
Vla.
Vc. Cb.
a 2

12
Fl.
Ob.
Fg.
Cor.(C)
Tr. (C)
Timp.
Vl.
Vla.
Vc.
Cb.
18
a2

24
Fl.
Ob.
Fg.
Cor.(C)
Tr. (C)
Timp.
Vl.
Vla.
Vc.
Cb.
30
a2

36
Vl.
Vla.
45
Vl.
Vla.
Vc.
Vc.
Cb.
Cb.
52
Fl.
Ob.
a2
Fg.
a2
Cor.(C)
Tr. (C)
Timp.
Vl.
Vla.
tutti
Vc.
Cb.

59
Fl.
Ob.
Fg.
Cor.(C)
Tr. (C)
Vl.
Vla.
Vc.
Cb.
a2
66

72
Fl.
Ob.
a2
p
Fg.
Cor.(C)
Tr. (C)
Vl.
Vla.
Vc.
Cb.
78
tr

84
Fl.
Fg.
1.
Vl.
Vla.
Vc.
Cb.
90
Fl.
Ob.
Fg.
1.
Cor.(C)
Tr. (C)
Timp.
Vl.
Vla.
Vc.
Cb.

96
Fl.
Ob.
Fg.
Cor.(C)
Tr. (C)
Timp.
Vl.
Vla.
Vc.
Cb.
102
Fl.
Ob.
Fg.
Cor.(C)
Tr. (C)
Timp.
Vl.
Vla.
Vc.
Cb.

109
Fl.
Ob.
Fg.
a2
Cor.(C)
Tr. (C)
Timp.
Vl.
Vla.
Vc.
Cb.
114
Fl.
Ob.
a2
Fg.
Cor.(C)
Tr. (C)
Timp.
Vl.
Vla.
Vc.
Cb.

120
Fl.
Ob.
Fg.
Cor.(C)
Tr. (C)
Timp.
Vl.
Vla.
Vc.
Cb.
126
Fl.
Ob.
Fg.
sf
sf
Cor.(C)
Tr. (C)
Timp.
Vl.
sf
sf
Vla.
sf
sf
Vc.
Cb.
sf
sf

132
Fl.
Ob.
a2
Fg.
Cor.(C)
Tr. (C)
Timp.
Vl.
Vla.
Vc.
Cb.
139
Fl.
Ob.
Fg.
Cor.(C)
Tr. (C)
Timp.
Vl.
Vla.
Vc.
Cb.

145
Fl.
Ob.
Fg.
Cor.(C)
Tr. (C)
Timp.
Vl.
Vla.
Vc.
Cb.
151
p
1.

158
Ob.
Fg.
Cor.(C)
Vl.
Vla.
Vc.
Cb.
1.
p
166
Fl.
Ob.
Fg.
Cor.(C)
Tr. (C)
Timp.
Vl.
Vla.
Vc.
Cb.
a 2
f

173
Fl.
Ob.
Fg.
Cor.(C)
Tr. (C)
Timp.
Vl.
Vla.
Vc.
Cb.
179
Fl.
Ob.
Fg.
Cor.(C)
Tr. (C)
Timp.
Vl.
Vla.
Vc.
Cb.

185
Fl.
Ob.
Fg.
1.
Cor.(C)
Tr. (C)
Timp.
Vl.
Vla.
Vc.
Cb.
192
Fl.
Ob.
Cor.(C)
Tr. (C)
Timp.
Vl.
Vla.
Vc.
Cb.

198
Fl.
Ob.
Fg.
1.
or.(C)
Tr. (C)
Vl.
Vla.
Vc.
Cb.
205
[♮]
a 2

212
Fl.
Ob.
Fg.
Vl.
Vla.
Vc.
Cb.
218
Fl.
Ob.
Fg.
Cor.(C)
Tr. (C)
Timp.
Vl.
Vla.
Vc.
Cb.
p
a2
tr

225
Fl.
Ob.
Fg.
Timp.
Vl.
Vla.
Vc.
Cb.
231
a2
Vl.
Vla.
Vc.
Cb.

237
Fl.
Ob.
Fg.
Cor.(C)
Tr. (C)
Vl.
Vla.
Vc.
Cb.
243
Fl.
Ob.
Fg.
Vl.
Vla.
Vc.
Cb.

250
Fl.
Ob.
Fg.
Cor.(C)
Tr. (C)
Timp.
Vl.
Vla.
Vc.
Cb.
257
a2

264
Fl.
Ob.
Fg.
Cor.(C)
Tr. (C)
Timp.
Vl.
Vla.
Vc.
Cb.
270
a 2

276
Fl.
Ob.
Fg.
a2
1.
Vl.
Vla.
Vc.
Cb.
282
Fl.
Ob.
1.
Fg.
Cor.(C)
Tr. (C)
Timp.
Vl.
Vla.
Vc.
Cb.

288
Fl.
Ob.
Fg.
Cor.(C)
Tr. (C)
Timp.
Vl.
Vla.
Vc.
Cb.
294

300
Fl.
Ob.
a2
Fg.
Cor.(C)
Tr. (C)
Timp.
[sim.]
Vl.
[sim.]
[sim.]
Vla.
[sim.]
[sim.]
Vc.
Cb.
307
Fl.
Ob.
a2
Fg.
Cor.(C)
Tr. (C)
Timp.
Vl.
Vla.
Vc.
Cb.

312
Fl.
Ob.
a2
Fg.
Cor.(C)
Tr. (C)
Timp.
Vl.
Vla.
Vc.
Cb.
318
Fl.
Ob.
Fg.
Cor.(C)
Tr. (C)
Timp.
Vl.
Vla.
Vc.
Cb.

323
Fl.
Ob.
Fg.
Cor.(C)
Tr. (C)
Timp.
Vl.
Vla.
Vc.
Cb.
sf
329
a2

335
Fl.
a2
Ob.
Fg.
Cor.(C)
Tr. (C)
Timp.
Vl.
Vla.
Vc.
Cb.
341
Fl.
Ob.
Fg.
Cor.(C)
Tr. (C)
Timp.
Vl.
Vla.
Vc.
Cb.

347
Fl.
Ob.
Fg.
Cor.(C)
Tr. (C)
Timp.
Vl.
Vla.
Vc.
Cb.
353
1
2

358
Fl.
Ob.
Fg.
Cor.(C)
Tr. (C)
Timp.
Vl.
Vla.
Vc.
Vc.
Cb.
368
Fl.
Ob.
Fg.
Cor.(C)
Vl.
Vla.
Vc.

377
Fl.
Ob.
Vl.
Vla.
Vc.
Cb.
f
384
Fl.
Ob.
Fg.
Cor.(C)
Tr. (C)
[f]
Timp.
[f]
Vl.
Vla.
Vc.
Cb.

390
Fl.
Ob.
Fg.
Cor.(C)
Tr. (C)
Timp.
Vl.
Vla.
Vc.
Cb.

396
Fl.
Ob.
Fg.
or.(C)
r. (C)
Timp.
Vl.
Vla.
Vc.
Cb.

402
Fl.
Ob.
a 2
Fg.
Cor.(C)
Tr. (C)
Timp.
Vl.
Vla.
Vc.
Cb.
408
Fl.
a 2
Ob.
Fg.
Cor.(C)
Tr. (C)
Timp.
Vl.
Vla.
Vc.
Cb.

413

Fl.
Ob.
Fg.
Cor.(C)
Tr. (C)
Timp.
Vl.
Vla.
Vc.
Cb.

418

Fl.
Ob.
Fg.
Cor.(C)
Tr. (C)
Timp.
Vl.
Vla.
Vc.
Cb.